Orchids and Neurons

Orchids and Neurons

Ellyn Peirson

Contents

Poet's Statement

I am a lover of oils and potions,
physics and metaphysics.
I seek patterns and meaning.
I create my own music and magic
from words and sounds and silence and shapes
and look for kindred souls
in the ruins of Pompeii.

We live on a planet that is a thin place - a place where time and infinity/light continually intersect. And yet we are taught to experience life as thick. When we move intentionally through the thickness that surrounds us and perceive Light, we can begin to punch peep-holes into and through Time.

This is my solitary 4-P journey... my journey with the partners of Prose, Poetry, Photography and Prayer. In my journey of Time and Light, I've learned that I can free myself from the ballast of ordinary Time and soar in the Light. This is Time Travel for me.

The most redemptive partner of my four is poetry. The process seizes me, and I become consumed by the emerging poem until it is complete. Poetry and prayer are closely related, at times with a loss of boundaries. That is why, I suppose, the sharing of poetry is an intimidating process.

For me, poetry is molecular and metaphysical. If it is not experienced in those two right hemisphere spaces, let it go. As T.S. Eliot said in "Tradition and the Individual Talent" in 1919,

The poet's mind is in fact a receptacle for seizing and storing up numberless feelings, phrases, images, which remain there until all the particles which can unite to form a new compound are present together.

It is my wish for you, my reader, that my Orchids and Neurons poetry touch you on a time-released level.

For the record, there are five poets who have deeply affected my feeling, thinking and writing – indeed, who I am – over many years of immersing myself in their work: William Blake, Gerard Manley Hopkins, Emily Dickinson, T.S. Eliot and Mary Oliver. Here is a stanza from the most brilliant wordsmith of all, Gerard Manley Hopkins, in "God's Grandeur." Let it play in the background of your right hemisphere as you read any poetry:

And for all this, nature is never spent;
There lives the dearest freshness deep down things;
And though the last lights off the black West went
Oh, morning, at the brown brink eastward, springs —
Because the Holy Ghost over the bent
World broods with warm breast and with ah! bright wings.

Lake Huron, the Bruce Peninsula, Ontario, Canada

milky way

Cry not over spilt milk and broken palaces
Weep not over bruised egos and cinch gardens
Mourn not our split personalities and crumbling terraces

Life is but a dream
Enter and awake

I. to each, wonderment

1. a brief history of strings

Mum. Lois. she started it all, home
pre-schooling (pre-natal?): mathematics, patterns, ante-
diluvianism (she loved that word), ESP, music, more dimensions and
more inabilities to play her music – remember the night
sky, she urges...

wink, wink...
theories chaos, quantum, fractals abound and we
vibrate, wink in and out of existence, with an impeccable
inherent code, attachment to
eternity within our own
DNA

think about it... the
parallel universes, the dense, winking
energy of other universes, senses beyond
five – light, wonder, true vision...

don't look away like that, go away like
that... with that
look...

symmetry, super-symmetry, elegance, eleven dimensions, the true
brain, vibrating strings, membranes, and brains
conceiving brains (universes), parallel
universes... if i could just slip through the
sunsetting horizon

multiplicity... another word she loved... did she
understand?
was that her
demon?
that she
understood?

look for the winking stars; we come
from beyond...

remember... remember the night, remember the
night sky...

she pulls the curtain back to see... and i no
longer exist

2. my father who art in heaven

oh yes, hallowed be thy name, my
fathermother. to others,
Frank. to me,
Dad.

still the background of my life, initially
you were the foreground. did you
know you were preparing me for a
deeper journey when we gardened
together? i, in a cardboard "nabob"
box; you lifting and moving me
around the hostile prairie
soil and explaining the below earth
sleep preparing baby seeds to break
forth.

precept giver: "grow in a purpose
of beauty and
usefulness." and,
"remember, little
Elly – to whom much is
given, much is
required."

pourer of footings: two blue spruce
trees to mark my birth; and music in
your clear, moving tenor
voice. while Lois in her pro
digious talent,
accompanied.

above all, you made God
real. you make God
real.

II. to each, a dream

3. orchids and neurons

Grief speaks quietly. hear it
for the beauty that's in it.

if we could see each
neuron as a mother cell,
the sheath
communicating, reverberating with
the music of
the spheres -
the colourshape of an orchid, her lips singing networks
over her columns and into other networks, leaving
stigmata behind. and only the composer can call and
harness this excitability into a concerto of sheer
beauty, knowing the
nuances
of the deliveries of incipiens mediam
finem. a lesson in the delicate strands - intimations - of
immortality.

Then and only then, when we understand
the lessons of orchids and neurons, will we see and be
healed. and everything -
everything -
will look as it never has
before...
the beauty essential to symphonies of
everything, where
orchid is brain and
neurons are pathways –

this is immaculate conception

4. ephemeral

white orchid
barely here, exquisite
translucency. breath of
angels and mirror of
other dimensions, perched in
the interval between, spanning
spanning now and
eternity with the breath and
fragrance of God.
ephemeral

when purple stands against the light
and blooms above the soft spring green,
she croons, this wistful purple sprite,
petals translucent, serene

the conversation, the soft garden talk of friends,
long after only the shadows and empty cups remained,
lingered over the table, mingling with the
scents of thyme and lilac...

5. the spring giveth

spring giveth and
autumn taketh away...
blessed be the doppelgängers root
ing and seeding silently below
life's surface, rest
ing for the coming spring's
birthings

6. make-believe on 3 levels

perhaps i am as they all say doing too much on my own
(maybe)
but it's such important business
(i feel)
being born
(headfirst)
with so many wrappedaround stringsattached that need
(severing)

and then there's the healing of that
(navel)
salute to old authority where i was to sacrifice
(self)
to others and live through other birthing independent growing
(progeny)
who know enough to be born early leaving me situated
(alone-naked)

the canal is blackwarm and slippery but i catch
(glimpses)
at the end. there's hardly room to get
(out)
without rippingbleeding pain and the need to redefine
(god)

those others who constrict clingclaw until my fleshbones
(ache-break)
my head and shoulders are in the light now of
(being)
fingers hands arms come next and then no one else can
(pushpull de-smear)

so that slimily and swimmingly i freely know that
(make-believe)
is to create my being intentionally in the truth of my new
(healingbirth)

7. nuances

I saw you
open and assailable last night
    sleeping
as you lay there in all your
toughly sought-out wrought-out
    defences

and your soul
opened up to me
and invited me into
    your dream

and i said yes
within the whisperings of sacred
    possibilities

as i stepped into
    your dream
in the fear born of awe
and love
    i saw you

as you never divulge

you turned
and from your mouth
streamed the riotous shades and sounds
    of our living
born of your breath

and so i became one
     with your breath
covered in a blanket of musical nuances
in the crook of your safe arm

and i remain there
carried along
on the multitudinous
colours and sounds
of love

knowing you as
     unassailable

8. rain radiance

she remains outdoors, yet
oblivious to the silvery deep greens and
darkened concrete...
as she walks uncovered brooding
at first unaware
    of the baptism.

slowly she dares to stay out, walk, embrace
slight smile shyly gone
as she sees
her self
    echoed in a puddle.

she steps over the evanescent image.

quite suddenly free –
    luscious liberation –

she feels the startling emancipation...

liberated to enjoy the countless pelting droplets
making fluorescent green in the grey
all around
too beautiful to be unembraced
because of fear, appearances.

warm and laughing
her clothes now obeying, conforming to her,
hair plastered to her cheeks and forehead,
this strange girlwoman in barefeet
    feels
in the ecstasy of deliberation
    herself in newness.

the understanding rain hangs in timelessness
from the leaves
    and she is a leaf
when time begins anew.

the minuscule prisms meld
    with her tears
running their course
as they fall sacrificially
    at her barefeet.

cleansed now
free but not understood by the
Dry.

    (de-liberation).

9. particles and collisions

ha! thirteen billion year old lightbulb,
microwave background of the
universe, harvesting and brewing
bluegreen primordial soup and throwing in
our galaxy's cosmic curds – why do they
curdle?

bang!

who is the master chef at the 'antediluvian light'?
who the sous chef?
who manages, listens, watches, stirs, directs?
temperature, stages, benign neglect, love applied and
withheld – all brought together in
precision to encourage the curdy bluegreen muck
to gain mass and volume and shoot off clusters of
newborn irradiated galaxies stewed by
the sun.

bang!

hallelujah! shout the archangels while
the heavenly host fly and sing to the
music of the spheres!

bang!
all, not merely a few, must see this and
abandon fear and whatifs – what if
i die?
what if
the planet dies?
drop fear and soar – there are so many
places to visit when
we leave.

hallelujah!

10. the deep colours of winter

when all seems white, colour
less, drab, and when the soul feels
barren,
find a way that is yours only. step
tentatively onto that path of grey,
pebbled with black and her murky
nuances. then rest, rest in all the drabness, the
monotony of fear. eyes, mind, ears tuned to
white. let the deep colours of winter
emerge on the screen, the fractal curtain
behind your eyelids. wait... anticipate
the astounding hues of the
continuum never found in our winterstate
of white rejection, our
flight
from it. listen for the rustling of newbirth at
the beyond edges paintsprayed with swatches of
birthing greens, reds, blues. do you hear the
meadowlark, the cardinal, the utterly beautiful
cry you've never heard. is it I, you will say...
and know... and the lavender, lilac, basil blends will
defy all before fragrances.
and as this thinplace, this
beautyspot, emerges, you will have found
the painted path home, pulling the alpha
and omega together. mark it with a
soulflag.
visit, embrace it with all trust when your time
comes.

11. change the dream

And did I hear you in the night -
tap, tap, tapping at the door
of my denial?

Come -
I heard you coax -
Come -
you whispered
until I couldn't stand
the din
knocking around in my head
flapping in my chest
exploding into my soul

Come -
you challenged -
To the tough part,
the slight curve in the road,
where the bluebells
become blooddrops
and the moss
becomes shrapnel

Come -
back to the belief of your pristine youth,
before it became smudged with comfort
and details
like the boredom of justification

Come -
and put your now easy words into action,
Walk in the land of torn children
I pull a grey blanket around my screaming panic
and look around - it was all a dream.
Turning the pillow over
I enter a gentler land of my new dreaming -
muffled, deaf

12. the arithmetic of war

Distortion-based Logic of implicit hypotheses
    thundering on and over in doubleproportions of doublespeak
Re-inventing Truth at every turn
    and turning it into Proofs
    and making angles out of angels

Logicide

Integers of War Games
raising ratings to see if anyone can wage the War Game
against CNN to the power of greatest
Fear and Addiction
    through the power of inversion

Lyricide

13. in the places where Infinity shines through

in the places where Infinity shines through reside
answers. destiny resides in finding them...
with inner vision, seeing
indigo at white cumulus borders, foaming
around Infinity's yawning presence. a simple
step of faith and i'm facing
Infinity's gaze; dappled
light shimmering on green blades. a simple
touch and i've stroked
Infinity's countenance; a shout of
raw despair—my God! my God! why?—and
Infinity transforms my tears into salve; a scream of
fury, jagged-edged, blade-slicing—You have
forsaken me!—modifies
modifies
moodifies
my
rage into sleep.

and i wake in silence—at last Silence—and
my head is clear... no more
words, shouts, tears take
possession and spin me into
anxiety, free-floating. instead a blanket of
Silence, holywarm—
comforting, comfort ye— i look
at it and see the warp and
woof of Infinity.

i find i can move now into
inexplicable encounters with a
storehouse of memories and
nowmoments; not alone but
accompanied
companied
by a Silence. a Silence i can
enter at will—i
take
my time.

and Joy begins to reveal
reveil herself in those
tentative entrances into
silent-moments
silence-choices, and i hear from
beyond
Silence,
an inaudible voice singing— I am
Infinity, the God of
despair and silence and
joy. I—the Infinite
Healer—heal
infinitely.

III. to each, a solitary journey

14. PILGRIM'S PROGRESSION

(VARIATIONS ON A THEME)
IN 5-7 TIME

PENTA

1. THE NEED FOR BEING
she knows her self well:
collective unconsciousness
yields her primal scream

2. RETURN TO SENDER
so he came first class
and left as printed matter
promising postcards

3. THE TWO BECOME TWO
she-he fell in love
primal scream and promises
never the two one

4. THE DIFFUSE FUSION
a child to cherish
link between past and future
fresh chance for freedom

5. HIDE IN THE RUSHES
let my children grow
give them a Mount Sinai walk
they need breathing space

SEPTA

1. CANADIANA
Mountain Prairie Sea
Eternity Images
Annihilation

2. THE PRAIRIE LILY
hair of golden wheat
her parents – hand-planted trees -
devour her feelings

3. EYESCAPE OF FLATNESS
train tracks, granary
plant the gold dust, knock it down
the caboose can leave

4. THE SOPHISTICATE
go East, young woman
an i begins to surface
formed by painful cries

5. SEASCAPE OF CRACKED MUD
dust, drought, slough, coulee
prairie dog drove her away
to smeared rain, blurred east

6. INSCAPE OF ROUNDNESS
profiles in concrete
lurid humid encounters
the loon calls her back

7. FOREVER LEARNER
she keeps her mind full
while soulsickness slumbers on
proof for more learning

PENTA

1. AN EPIPHANY
the Star leading her
through black valleys to bright hills
Creation's Maker!

2. COMMENT ON CONFLICT
Marx contradicted:
leave the opiate behind
proletarian

3. LOVE WORKS TOGETHER
peace like a river
flows past her understanding
but all for her good

4. LOVE TO A DAUGHTER
wallpaper, she asked -
do you write on anything? -
only if it helps

5. AN ETERNAL WHY
and is there a god?
Caring Dispenser of Love
inspire me to life

15. lessons learned from nature

harmony isn't soft and placid
harmony is easy borders,
a beautiful, varied constellation of parts,
bringing into your life colours and origins,
a passion for movement within the laws.
let harmony reign in the free world -
be wild with kindly tolerance...
it's what we're here for.

16. in that brief gesture

friendships based on rhododendron trees – soft
pink, almost invisible against the broad leaves – and
solid stolid torso extending arms to
bond shapes to forms,

are robust.

the friends perceive.
blossomkisses
offered
received
reciprocated
now hand-in-hand the friends reach
out to the rhododendron tree, and
in that brief gesture eternity is created,
circle-completion in the timeless garden of
rhododendron trees and friendships

17. an apron awaiting

I think of his mother's kitchen today
the one that raised her shoe-living children because
of her talent, that farming talent of
preserving and baking and cooking
for sixteen children and
two parents and
who knows who else

and he was the eldest, the big
brother to all of them and then came
his sudden graduation to fill-in
father when the real
father died
so young

and now, my friend, you've managed the
final graduation with grace and
ease
that impermeable made
permeable at the perfect time for
you and not
us

shall we gather at the
river now –
say, at 2 today and
wave to the
other side?

until it's my time, dear friend...

18. for my daughters

(for Rebecca, Monica)

just a little laneway in Lisbon
everyday
notice these things:
the little path beside your dream,
the past that clings,
this moment that calls you upstream
where lights play

everyday
shake off your dream; stand naked; free;
clothe yourself in the green of destiny
love first, think second, drop fear
now see the birthdream, invisible, clear
where lights play

19. if I stop

when you walk, do you listen?
and do you see?
this is about soulhearing and
soulseeing.

and do you stop, so as to
commune... comprehend?

I heard a robin today, not very high
above me. I stopped. the happiest robin I
have ever heard – burbling, singing (the
Hallelujah Chorus as a solo), laughing –
jubilantly proclaiming, *rejoice! re-
joice! for the world is good, and so are
you!* I looked up again and saw that the robin
was light – or more correctly that its
words were... a glorious white light, so
white that parts of it, as it hovered above
me, were blue. it furled and rolled and
tumbled over and under itself. and I understood –
I understood that the original state of the human
heart is love and goodness and the capacity to be
light. and more than anything, I desired my words and
thoughts and actions to be original. and in a
soulflash I grasped that I might disappear if
I could possibly sustain
the state. I beamed a lightsmile up
to my robin.

in this joy, this bliss, this original
state, I looked down and saw
a sunny, orange daylily. its surprisingly
resilient petals, fluttering in the soft breeze, sent out bursts of
petaldust in celebration for my interpreting the language of
common birds and ordinary flowers.

all because i
stopped.

20. not by my choice

[based on Ruth 1:16-17 KJV]

do not leave me; and never
ask me to leave you except that
I die first

that is the order
and an order

and so I again demand – do not
leave me
and cease to say – do you
hear me? - cease to say that I
must not follow.

I must. I have
no choice

for whither thou goest, I will go;
and where thou lodgest, I will lodge:
thy people shall be my people, and thy God my God
for
ever and for
ever.

where thou diest, will I die,
in the flash of light and renting of time
there will I be dead in the
instant of your soon last breath, singing
the song I always sang to you at
the foot of the goldenhead bed

this moment perpetuated
until my final following of
you

the Lord do so to me, and more also,
if ought but death part thee and me.

do not go – this is a plea, a demand, a
favour, shall we say?

the order is wrong, so very
wrong.

I pray God make it right.

21. did I believe you were coming back?

every autumn, now approaching the
fourth in my via dolorosa,
I wonder if I'll see you, as the year begins
to wind
down. spin
off.
when the colours and fragrances you cherished
remind
rewind me and rustle up
death
in the beginning gentle
crunch and powdering of
leaves.

22. efficient readiness

i don't much care anymore for any
thing other than every thismoment. my
choice now to relish, plunge, sing,
agonize as thismoment
requires of me.

you see—i understand the need to
travel home. to be
ready, packed lightly with mostly
light... and desire... yes, desire, urgency,
anticipation, excitement. after all the
trips beginning and ending in waiting for
battered luggage with red bows—that's
mine!—to be spat
out upon carousels, i'm ready for the
ultimate.

the trip home requires no
thing other than every
thing released; every part parcel
particle of what seemed important, like
success, cast-off shredded discarded. and
possessions, now things reduced to
efficient beauty, the slickest in
function.

this readiness is good and true. it's a
readiness that waits expectantly in the
background of my
good, for the most part, life. although one
friend worried until i fully
explained.

it comes without stringsattached—except
one
one which i beseech in utter
earnestness. and goes like this
i simply ask in a stripped
down minimal way—may i
please be there to welcome those i
birthed and their
offspring
?

it's no more than any
parent would ask. i would hope that
You, Parent Force and Lover of my
Soul
would understand. after
all—You were there to welcome
Yours.

(forgive me, for i
presume too much.)

my suitcase is packed.

23. a bearable sadness

Now that I've found you,
Now that I know
with the clarity of glass -
I see, I see
that the dancing light that encircles you
requires that I gaze from a distance -
a galaxy away

and wait
with the patience of Job
and the love of Venus
over here in the crooked corner
of my burning love
that moves and dissolves
with the very rhythm of my heart's blood
coursing and cursing
my ethereal position

I would touch you
if I could
but we are separated by
ages that become black eons
and
positions that roar and resound
back to us and off the walls of this
world of rigidity and
blasting judgments

in perceptions that are off
by dazzling light years

resting pulse rate

so I wait
and I touch, without your
body and
light-sensitivity knowing,
although I know your soul knows
what you might not -
the resounding
meteoric truth

hurtling its way here
spinning
with fragments falling in a separate dance
that must be our lives here
and not our life here -
showering tinsel and rock
fossils of what our life was like
in that distant galaxy
that was home

and that will be

so, for the duration
I wait
and let our souls commune
in those visits we cannot remember
except as purple dreams

an equal sadness
a bearable sadness

24. About

In the end
it's about
love and now and nothing in between
and everything in between and constancy even
in roiling grief

In the end
it's about
you
and me
and what we've created together and if

we can stay the storm
by seizing its power to conceive, deliver
ourselves, pressed down and running over
as one
even in division

In the end
it's about us
and the babe we have created in
our luscious garden green, and in
the very air we exude

In the end
it's about entwined stiffer fingers
a reeking oneness—
one heart shared
one soul inhabited

In the end
there is no one left but
our history, the book we've written
and all that's
miraculous

IV. to each, offered healing

25. old enemy

a line appears snakelike
    and stretches out before me
        i turn around to see it
            stretch just as thinly behind
        i haven't noticed the line before
    in all my scramblepace slumbernot

and now i recognize it
        in a flash of vividsight

it is that continuum called   Time
            between birth and death
                where there is much
            called Gripping
        by the fingernails

that continuous old archenemy
    serpent to first others
        stretches thinly powerful
            in my gone and to be

        it stops just short
            of the horizon

26. Nativity, in fragments

I think of Christmas now in
fragments... a fragment. I realize this is the
gift of Christmas – fragments of an in
comprehensible gift. A gift of approximation
to stained glass, an ex
quisite, multicoloured, massive stained
glass window beyond
imagination...
and a rock comes, a
comet. hurtling through the uni
verse and pushing

And when that ex
plosion, that in
vasion happens the speed of light is
shattered and the sound barrier is
smashed. And the unbearable noise of
cosmic laws colliding with the force of the
universe is so great that shepherds fall down
and see angels and a baby is delivered so
roughly in a stable. Some report hearing the
music of the spheres just as I now hear
light songs without words in no language, no
language except over and over and over dona
nobis pacem until I realize it's being sung by our
departed son in his once upon a time soprano
voice and look!
look! I am a vessel of light

hearing the chorus of my cloud of witnesses – father,
mother, sister, son, and the one who left today. May
I join your chorus? Could we sing as we sang at home on
the stony cold Canadian prairie? bleak… mid… and the
light comes again and I see I am holding a shard of stained
glass and over there in that playground at the edge of light, that
winter light seeping in through the broken stained glass
step through the light, do away with time

consider the mysteries of existence

I come from light and will
return to light… the
interval is the dream

27. lenten yellow

in the scratched grocery store bucket,
deceptive sophistication, the yellow tulip
yearns. it
reaches out – immortalize me, all ye who
labour and I will give you rest for your
soul. you yearn, too – from your own
scratched
bucket. desire and empty
ness collide,
immortalize me. forever make me
yours and I will give you rest. reciprocity, the recip
rocity of beauty and heavy-laden
ness. how will you keep my

greens in myriad shades and not let
them droop and fall flat against some glass
vase – perhaps lalique, translucent green with
dancing goddesses pressed in and running
over – and how
will you notice and nourish my yellow flower, kissed with
the red of God's lips? will you
hear Haydn playing his sonata #29 in the back
ground – so sadly light and airy, the chaconne of
the yellow tulip red-tinged, tulipred, crimsonred. chaconne of the
son's
blood, second Isaac. for it is
now Lent. and I am but

another Christ to be slain... this is my body, this is
my blood given, my tulipblood, for you. take
and see that i am another sacrificial
lamb. you stare and wonder (others have been
crueler) – will you buy, a few palm branches perhaps
for effect, that table possibly or a window... take me into your home
heart, paint me into
canvas for a generation to say, my mother painted that lovely
little still life (still, still with me when purple breaks)... she had a
nice talent... that's why I keep it, keep it, heysanna hosanna, green
grow the palm trees, oh!

you bend and we look eye-to-eye... i see your soul... open
up, take me in, understand this lent is for you, this greater love is
because of you. and your lens closes. you
step back and open your designer bag.

digitalclick. Lent downloaded. and you go on your palm-branches
strewn heysanna way.
oblivious, loveblind...
and yet...
you have another chance, chances are
limitless.

see me in the resurrection that is coming – and i will come again in
the new bursting and melodious garden where red buds
sing and birds, green and purple, write music for all who are
heavy-laden... yellow symphonies and violet nocturnes to be
played wherever spring creates its perpetual in
surrection
and...
over there...
beside that large impalpably pulsating
stone, i am
born again

28. Lenten Rose

on the Friday in its goodness,
where each drop of browblood became a
potion. for some
poison; for some
balm; for some
health; for all
love...
each drop be
came a
hellebore, the Gethsemane
Garden of Lenten
Roses.

29. ode to Auden

(as I walked out one evening)

nature awakes. as it must in Solstice, to
accommodate the longest night. we respond in
tinseltrading - drawn-in, hood-
winked by Saturnalia flair. and yet, in tender
repetition

mother comes, slicing through
time, precision-lasering, ener-
gizing the dull, the dismal,
(banishing them briefly) and
slapping awake the faces of slumbering botany and
the cellular memories, vibrant memories of the
mindheart, dearheart, until we sense the
coursing of blood through our veins. we notice
you, at last,
in the red surges of our surroundings.

we feel it, this
happiness, this joy, these
good tidings in our re-birthing, re-bonding
with you as
the winter sun, midwife to all solitary
reincarnations. the radiations, arms carrying
gifts of swaddling clothes, tear through
intuitions buried in
time. in the slow darkness come the
arousal and fluttering of angelwings, the holy
spectral, heavenly host of reds and yellows
and blues, smudged with royal purple.
flushed-fleshed out anew, our
spirits move, awakening –
our first love, primal number of all
computations, given freely in the
shadowshades of
the deep solstice.

we turn to face our
glorymarch, agree to trudge toward Lent's lavender *(?)*, calling
from the Ides of time, over there in the womb-forest.
we see, dimly, in the distance the fresh nativity, the shapes, forms –
delivery rooms of
rebirth when mothersun
rematerializes at the sacredspring
sunrise

30. this is a photograph of grief

(for Glenn, with thanks to Margaret Atwood's poem)

if i were ever to sit down
with my
grief—invite her in for fenugreek tea and an
iced cupcake—
and let her talk to
me, i would
succumb...
to madness, though,
not death the
preferable. if the

photograph she would take should happen to
show the negative of the tea—grey grief and i sipping, she
with the white gloves and jackie-o
hat, i looking down at my sneakers, reassured i
can run... should you see us together in the
photograph as negatives, ghosts so to
speak, please
delete

photographs of grief keep the
subjects trapped in
timegloom

and so i won't ever let her in to
elaborate when she shakes my hand
wrought,
tear
wrought
iron door; no i will continue to
swallow, brace, grit
my teeth—how grief
craves enamel!—and
shut down. i will
continue to find the
fork in the road where
route one is now and
route two is nausea.

no—when grief
yawns, slurps, wakens
ravenous—when she turns from
the camera and clings to the dank corners and
dark edges of the photograph—i will
remember only the visceral check
list: your nuances,
your voice in all its
modalities, your
face, your
eyes—and i must stop
there, com
press the beauty i
so trustingly
conceived, delivered into life, and i must go
to the fork to make one of two
choices for the day's travel, with no stops for visiting old
photographs.

31. rooms and roses

in my daughter's garden
are many rooms and
roses and fragrant herbs, her
green thumb a green hand, her
soul
privately revealed.

after all, that's what gardens are, the
revelation of the gardener's soul.

in this one, the maintenance of per
haps the first garden, say close to
eighty years ago. "typically Toronto!"
The shed, tidy and well
kept like a mother in a granny flat, a
very old mother. is she still in there?
partially.

against the new privacy fence, necessary
because the old neighbours loudly
quarrel in Italian with a touch of
English, is the old,
still working Portuguese cooker.

a carefully laid stone path wends its way down
the centre from here to the shed, and the garden on
either side is filled with flowers and bushes and
vegetables... I'm waiting for luscious
tomatoes.

I sit under the lavish grape arbour, protected
from the hot sun and clear azure skies. Puffs of
white clouds drift lazily by in the rhythm they
hear from another dimension.

Her herbs decorate the stairs – big pots
brimming with green herbs, so brimming
I want to take them to market, "singing
basil and rosemary, alive, alive-oh! take
a little cilantro in your hand and crush it. buy
it and rosemary and oregano... you'll need all
this for the soon tomatoes!"

Let me paint the picture i already see before
me, across the patio... for she does this – she makes
pictures in her garden. This one, to complete
her garden is against the privatized chain link fence –
yellowized.
on the left, as we look, a ladder against the fence,
and in the middle, a pretty old wooden table... did
someone make bread on it once? I would have.
in the centre a rustic pot, home to plants, and
leaning against it, a small, beguiling painting, a
harbour in blues and greens, boats and clouds. and
best of all, an old yellow fishing boat, reefed and matching
its yellowized background. A navy blue bicycle on the right
completes the picture, industrial.

robins and cardinals call. a chainsaw complains in the far distance,
cigarette smoke wafts over the back fence.

This is the Toronto garden.

This is my daughter's soul.

32. vespers

hush
weeping
citrus slices
evening glow
soft sun and
languid lake
water joins sky
and sunset says farewell to swaddling echoes of a day
the time of silence and voices heard below the horizon
breathless
drowning
in ancient
lovers and
lifetimes of
visitations
calling me
beyond to
unborn
melody
resting
place
past
my brain
seductive
conception

33. DREAMING

And if I break the dream
smash it and pick up the shards
of spun glass
and send them spinning into the clouds
until they are shredded
and scattered into the bleeding corners of my heart

will you be there?

will you be there
when I die to that ancient dream
I've inhabited for false eternities
in crystal and ice, immovable, imperceptible -
will you be there?

in the new light
that you love in its sun-hardness
seeping in through a western window
in the late afternoon
will you be there

to take me home?

34. the truth of the rose

I gaze at your beauty and I'm numb
I cannot describe it... I stare and I notice
the innumerable folds, circles, softness, colours,
fragrance and am spellbound until
I am drawn again to the epicenter of your
gaze. "I am obsessed with completions" he
once said... the one I lost and must find.

And I know
this is vital – I play with
something fundamental, Platonic... I have always let
the truth of the rose prevail, while I flee from the invitation
she offers... "come with me, into my gaze" she smiles, "and I will
take you to the machine shop of truth, beauty, goodness,
where the great master of the universe demonstrates his
carpentry of souls, new and damaged, until they shine and fly to
their rightful place. And, all the while, the fathermother
from some nearby room sings the truth of the
universe and blesses, while the spirit, the holiest spirit
soars – goes and comes, comes and goes to the machine
shop, releasing souls to the brotherson's carpentry for
repair and delivery to new homes.

"Oh, do come," the beautytruth urges, "you do not have to
stay. Come for a vision. There have been few since John and
Hildegard. You'll see so much you can't put into your words (all
words are understood here). It will live wordless in your soul,
sustaining you."

She sings songs hymns in praise of the absolutes of the universe –
    O come and see your home of many mansions...
    starsborn, infinity, black holes
    eclipses, full moons, setting suns
    meteors in verdant greens and fullblooded reds
    sprinkling this milkyway
    O come and kneel...
and fades away...

I step to that dark abyss, the centre, and
dive.

35. lightseekers

I had a dream last night infused with an apocryphal light – a dream of
the ravaging, rock-hewn power of
multiple gods—
gods blind to anything but power
and their piteous, radical servants in bunkers, sending their lambs to
slaughter, with orders to keep boots in the air and
carnage on the ground...

repetition compulsion

until I saw a vessel – great in size and light and immense
in quiet splendour, a vehicle, cru
cible – beauteous lightseeker and lightgiver, finding
holding dispensing light to the
lightlookers. the ones whose very souls
perceive the light, the truth – the seek and you
shall find ones whose souls are becoming
visible. for they shall find, free on the streaming
beams the exquisite endurable ache of ultimate
consumption, becoming one with the
light.
radiated.

and then I saw great waters parting and joyful wavelets clapping in
delight, singing the song of
what is, what was and what is
to be... a metaphysical world, disembodied
holiness: Original

V. to each, a great womb

the Great Womb

Lake Huron:

- has four sisters – Lake Ontario, Lake Erie, Lake Michigan, Lake Superior;

- has the longest shoreline of the Great Lakes – 3,827 miles;

- is the second largest of the great lakes by surface area;

- is the third largest by volume of water;

- has a surface area is 23,000 square miles (59,600 square kilometers);

- has a volume is 850 cubic miles;

- has 30,000 islands,

- embraces Manitoulin Island, the world's largest freshwater island.

Great Gitche Manitou said:
I have made you great, O Huron Waters, and I have made for you four equally great sisters. And when the White Man comes in a few eons, he shall marvel and believe he has found his way to the next sea. And you and your sisters will roar and roil in laughter at the White Man's blindness. And I say unto you, do not let him stay, for he will demonstrate no understanding of Oneness.

36. best vantagepoint

Sparkling mirrorlake
serene
brilliant
rippleless

Sentinels of
rock
and
leaning evergreen
Stand guard
mute, knothole vision
Protectors

Seductive mirrorlake
Ice Woman looks
on -
undulating image yields mystery smile
in return
cool-brilliant, prescient
mirthless

Shatterproof mirrorlake
Ice Woman looks
through -
clearview to the bottomcold
birthless

She moves to the marker
Nailed, heart-hole
No diving
Sailcraft only

Unchurned, she returns to her gazepoint
The dumb loon slips by
returngazes
laughs
and
vanishdives.

37. pray me a lake

sometimes monochromatic in its heavyhaze,
although usually scalpel clean, the
excision between sky and lake in shades of blue and
green – new shades of monochrome; nothing
on the horizon; nothing on the
horizon but pain.

nothing on the horizon but beauty and
anxicty...

it must be divine, dear, for you to have your slice of lake
huron blueberry pie, sitting on the deck of the
day... sunning... reading... cooling
off in the water – the great lake, honey! With the kids old
enough now to be in
dependent. Oh, I'd love to visit for a while.

and my head says to me, if only you
knew, darling…
if only you could see me reading and conjuring up
buddhas and killing them on the sheldon kopp
road to deep water.

after much grit and patience, I recognize I know the sound
of one leg kicking as the gurgle of drowning and so I
swim and swim and swim – multiple strokes until I
realize I love this lake and she
loves me and I learn the battle is always
within the self.

lake huron accepts my gifts of grief, letting them sink –
I am born again from this womb, loved, free,
healed. I swim toward
the flaming red horizon as unreachable as a
rainbow…

It is a hopkins sky, "shining with shook foil" and suffused with
"brooding" utter
protection.

38. spring flower

Behold!
I am the Indian Paintbrush,
The first to blossom -
iridescent and fiery red -
After a bleak winter.

I seemed not to be there
nor was God -

And then came my Springtime
when the seemingly withheld
Kiss of God
burst through my fears
reviving
invigorating
pulsing
until I could
resist no longer.

I push up
brilliant
robust
where growth seems impossible
from among rocks
and hear
the ecstasy of nature
melodious
miraculous
and loose my fears
into
the arms
of
re-creation

39. inclination

Hey stranger, she said.
(He inclined his head.)
We walked today as we never have before,
through cooling woods, down rock steps, and to the shore
of great Lake Huron, cold upon cold,
like our hearts -
roaring, reaching out to touch and hold.

Hey stranger, she said.
(He inclined his head.)
Did you hear the sweet songs of love
the long lapping of passion?
Did you see the newborn flowers
the strange forces that fashion
the beauty of the white subtle,
the mutilation of the black obvious
as between us?
or were the dead fish,
the water-smoothed rocks
the poison ivy
more curious?

Hey stranger, she said.
(He inclined his head.)
Myriad long brief years have lived and died in day and night as ours,
While love has been washed up to bleach or blossom with the flowers
of our silence, on a nebulous blue horizon out there where we stagger
in the sun and the stars and the haze of togethers we share.
    I understand, he said.
    (She inclined her head.)

40. Good Friday at the Great Womb

Hunting, searching for something, anything
in the words and forms
Gestures and gesticulations
genuflections

I find it instead
in the creaking and groaning
of the ice on the lake
in the trickle and sparkle
of newborn rivulets
in the whistle of the cardinal
and the trill of the red-winged blackbird
in the sun's laying hands on
my furrowed brow

And in my neighbour who needed
comforting.

41. the numen

I saw Lake Huron
take a long, slow slurp
of the sun tonight -

swish and savour it
over and under its
inky tongue -
indigo ingesting fire

red wine was never like this
and I knew that
if I could have
moved
at the speed of light

I would have stepped through
the molten crack into
a Parallel Universe

42. the loons have been and gone

The loons have been and gone this weekend—
Mergansers, Canada Geese—shedding autumn;
Some asking me to join them—but this is not my time.
I gaze over the steely, fall blue of Lake Huron
and see
Stonehenge, Atlantis pathways
and turn back to Spindrift, drizzled.

I hear you... all of you...
laughter, shrieks, secret murmurs, intense opinions bracketed by
louder articulations of rowdy disagreement, and loudest is the brood-
ing silence, split crossways by our looniness—and love. And I see
you... all of you... who grace this sanctuary—you swim, read, eat,
play, chatter, cry, sleep—and love—
your lingering forms move around and about
at will
and come
to the always-smoldering
firepit of stories and songs
punctuated with cloudy dots of marshmallows

and I see the one
who came but twice
not re-welcomed in her
tumult, bedlam, incessantness—
her roiling wake

and i the mourning dove
see her spirit and we
glide by
each other
touch wing to wing

passing, our alwayspassing
never stayinglong in that passing—
each having opposite directions to take
always

farewell, mother of my earthbirth
free now in the skies and stars you yearned for
always

I miss you
as I always have.

43. how do i love you, lake huron?

How do I love you? Let me count the ways.
I love you to your horizon and beyond
Where my soul is healed, we have our bond In my
Being's birth and my ending's blaze.

I love you to the setting of everyday's
Sun and rising of moonbeam and starshine.
I love you Onely swimming in your wine
and wildly when your sky divides the waves.

I love you completely with ancient and new
Grief subterranean, comforted with each new rod.
I love you with a love I find as God
While you sustain me, cover me blue,

Embodied in your molecules – I will
Return to your love when city life is still.

44. railing against god and gods and huronsons

troubled troubling turmoiled
i consulted with Lake Huron today – what
shall I do, great womb? with my
turmoiltrouble, my grief, my
god – oh both of you with your con
founded reflections – stop!
stop reflecting and tell me, tell
me what to do with you
both while i rail against you
both with colours and screams and
my floundering in the water   must
i scream?

listen... listen... list first to the
music... the vivace in the waves second con
certo... in the
spindrift where the
bows flail against the strings like
you do now... see... see.. seize first to the
colours while your digitalizing flails a
gainst the horizon where lies
always the answer – in on the horison, the son
of man and woman... do you not
remember the contrapuntus, the art of
the code of all masters, the god of
all gods, the art of the
fugue

45. the storm

Lowering, scouring
clouds, black indigo, creampurple—churning. some this way, some
that;
heavingwaves become gleaming silverschools of flashing fish
in whirlpools swirlpools. we, only vapours,
cower—colourless, at a scaredstill

and then we go out, you and I, and inhale the dense electric air in
her Eye
point, frame, shoot digital, scamper to the Great Lake's Edge
digitalclicks—digitalchicks
Boomcrack. Hurryback.
greatdrops smack. and we lick them—stormtaste
and we love this Great Lakeforce imbibing us
the heavens open—gods thunderspeak
we close the door, pull up a chair, faceout upon
echobooms of Jupiter and Mars. thunderstruck

VI. to each, journeys within journeys

46. colours from the Portuguese

when did the universal force contrive to
hover over Lisboa? why were clouds diminished –
colours exaggerated? was Merlin left here... or a few
druids... a leftover Phoenician? the archaic sorcerer engraves
brains from a crucible conceived in Light
of chaste whites, innumerable greens, Azulejo blues and citrus
borders. the sorcerer steps back, takes a broad paint
brush and dips into the crucible. now is the time of splashing the thick
oils of
October's magenta bougainvillea riotously into the already etched
colour
carvings in the brain...

and the mind is so hypnotized, the psyche so
dazed that no
one can bond, send down roots into this ancient city of
illusions. traveller or resident, it matters not, trudges the
hills, walks the pavement waves... unaware that no feet ever
connect with what seems to be there. rather

all is swept away by bedazzling colours. predestined –
everything spills into
the old Tagus... and all of it, all of it... empties into the
sea, the home of all portuguese.

47. the healing

no wonder, is it, that Emily wrote about the sea
parting to reveal another sea and so on until per
haps infinity is understood

and no wonder, then, is it that I have felt all my life
the sea in my gut... longing for something somewhere some
how - a true home, not those childhood brutal prairies

that rush of angst, loss of boundaries, sitting on the top
of a little hill crying help me help me help! afraid to look
down, over to see the sea. when I finally got there

to where I could see no end, taste salt and her stories, gag on beryl
brine and float on sapphire's surface – and discover, perceive that
this anguish becomes rest, soothed by mothersea

48. faceless god of the dank grotto

Caput Mundi, head of the world! praise be to your
layers and layers of dead gods – headless, faceless works of
stone. broken. Roma, still offering myths –
gods at war and twins shewolf-suckled, but no
perception that the wolf just might have been god –
no salutation. no credit. head of stone.
lapis caput mundi. faceless (inferus) head.

faceless god of the dank grotto. templed forever. palatined
forever. dying by the miniscule movement of
drops of water. sculpted rock succumbs to the primeval, re-
lentless water dial, time-keeper in
darkness.

49. through the eyes of the Pantheon

we are the gods, invented in your image. cap
tured by you and im
prisoned in the perfection of this structure
allowing movement of truth in and
out. and so by our eyes -
the eyes of all gods you have
created who move at will -
pantheon
find pan aletheia, that spirit of truth
available only at the moment of the door
way into death.
immortal divisible invisible
singularity and expansion
shhh... listen... cosmic burst -
a plethora of eyes

50. la Serenissima 1

as quietly as the soft lap of the water against the wall of a canal
as gently as the touch of ancient voices
night descends until
there is that moment, that
hush, that
breathlessness between then and
now and the lights of
Venetian night life

51. la serenissima 2

Cannaregio. an ordinary street in an
ordinary neighbourhood. i walk toward
the lagoon, the mysterious, the extra
ordinary. on my pilgrimage to the vessel, the
vaporetto, the allegro con ordinario, upon which
i shall splash my way to the dwelling place of my
God. and free myself into the holy. through the lagoon.
faint signs of the Dolomites
a blessing through the lagoon to Torcello. i shall find
my God there where Venice started... where i arose from
seaweed and sent Attila running.

I look around this ordinary
street. drawn to look up, i am
transfixed, mortified. for i see the holy there –
in the ordinariness of the Venetian decay, the oddly
chosen everyday flowers and the common vileness of
electric wires. eels.

and yet, the shrine is tended carefully lovingly… the Christ child
reaches for the saint's face, flowers and book also in
saintly hands… but what is it I see, what am I missing
it is the gaze, the shared gaze, the icon
that I want. devotion. mutual. holy.
What do the carved words say?

CONF. MASCHILI
S. VINCENZO
DE PAOLI

I acknowledge the holy in this ordinary –
inscription along Venetian
streets. below the shrines so carefully, lovingly

created.
ad sanctam vitam in ordinariis.

my journey began before I was born.

52. la serenissima 3

MOTHERSEA

Marco—Polo! Aero—Porto!
I dive lagoondeep
strokespeed through fluorescent green; sweeping tendrils gather me
    to return me to Atlantis. subterranean
No! I must return to the
    dream of all dreams, with digital camera. waterproof

stroke, breathe... expire. Inspire to Inspiration
Leaving weedswept bodies in islandsunk

I must return to domes and filigree
where violins sing themselves into mosaics
    and plaster their notebodies against angelvaulted heavens
where gilded gondolas slip into mute backwaters
    and sometimes slit the silverthroated moon

I swim... past Torcello's pale towers of archaic
    husky, howling voices screaming against
the Huns, and later, later—birthing sighbridges over malarial torpor

great solitude of solitudes. past sunken boatloads of corpsesplagued
and San Michele's bonesapart behind hostile cedarwalls—
    bonescrying soulsdying... dispatched by the Bonaparte

Imagination's jewel emerges seizing
       my imagination—brainwaves of waterwaves
turquoise upon indigo, aqua upon seamills of my mind, mindstroke
seastroke... to the glittering saintencrusted piazzas

breaststroke... reststroke. plunge and risebreathe.
lungsburst, heartfelt
home, the Republic's pureform—where nothing is—
until I find lions and ocelots in mosaics
and in fretworks worrynots of pink palaces and mahogany violins

I'll stay for another day or two, and perhaps another lifetime
       under the Rialto for daysleep, and in the slinking of nightdream
I'll swim murky canals, mythhunt. and cross the bridges in my head

Finally shall I go out to the Lido to play
only then shall I reclaim my gills, shed long ago at watersedge. and
sink deep deep into the seabosom. my home of watermilk and
aqualove
       and attachments wrought in bonedeep oceans

       Atlantis regained.

VII. to each, the call home

53. my soul, wait in silence for God only

Listen to me!
I said -
    Listen!

How much longer
    do I have to wait?

Listen!
    to me!

I see you
    high and lifted up -
Back turned -
    in all your robes
    of glory
Turn around!

Get off that cloud
    of Almighty nothingness
And speak!

    Tell me you love me -
Take away my burning
    fear of extinction.

What more can I do
        to get your lofty attention?
I've raised my voice
        and my fist
Demanded, begged
        coerced, beseeched.

I yield!

I might just as well
        throw my soul
        against your
Sacred Abandonment
        and noiselessness

        the Emptiness of Nothingness

Pardon me?

Hurtling, blasting, bursting
        Soaring
        Blissing
        Neverending
Through the gates of Heaven,
        over the ancient ramparts
of silence, guilt, and racket –

And into Infinity
        wordless........

54. thin places

(remembering Margaret)

When my time comes,
when I find the thin place waiting only for me
May I slip through
leaving breath
    here
to pick up breath
        there
my expire becoming my inspire
like the sun sinking into the mouth of the sapphire sea
round
hefty
radiant

And may the little ozone hole I leave
in earthy membrane
close fast and
tightly to a rowdy
welcome

And may I be pulled in by the same arms
that took you from mine
while I mid-wifed to keep
	your shell here

And shall we dance and spin—free again—
through the white sheets and greenest fields
of our Cosmos-home?
laughing in uni
song again
	again
		again

55. no longer lying down

there comes a time
when the innocence and privilege of good health falter.
there comes a time when you finish shouting and
railing against all that's good and just.
there comes a time when that crooked fork in the
shadowy trail seems to coax...
which direction, my little one, pretty one...
where are you going, my loved one?
come this way with faithÍ¾ go that way into the
slough of despondency
your choice and
you can do it
at the fork of singularity and random mutations.
there comes a time when you stand up and shout at the blank, un
yielding heavens,
"I'll be damned if I'm going to take this lying down!"
there comes a time when all the cancerwords you know need
to be uttered, written, thrown against the blankness
and you fight back with your whole
army of
options
will and
intent
with the artillery of words and the cannon of
unrelenting connection to life and
Love.

and then there comes a time when that road is
for you

56. white midnight.

I can go back to bed now -
the snowstorm is over, it
seems somehow gentler now with no
white-outs and no traffic, no
feet crunching in the too early winter -
too drastic...

I choose instead to see the pure white as
fallen blooms of alabaster magnolia, and
wilted white hydrangea mixed with florets
of ivory lilac ...
so I shall return to my white pillows and sheets, to
sleep's lullaby and in
the new morn waken in the dim memory
of my dream. I'll run outside to
remember. and then I shall
scoop up the petals of
mingled snowflowers and get drunk
on their white perfume

I waken, remembering, sensing the alchemy of
sweet perfume, white flowers mingled in the
crucible of the snowstorm... whence is that
goodly fragrance? I eagerly throw open my
window, tear at its allegorical shutters and slash
the curtain between the
ordinary and the
holy...
knowing I will see coatings of white surplices and under
stand the goodly pigment and fragrance of
winter with the eye of
God.

And I see,
I see how
the Divine Painter loves the
cold north with its ploughed
streets and banks of layered sur
plices, frozen life dotted here and
there with red and green people taking
control of snow to allow
ordinary tasks. I am home where I am
destined to be, swaddled in the holy garments of
God. I pause my clattering head, accepting
the gift of perfect

Quietude.

Yuletide.

57. the eye of the iceberg

alive again
from the frozen silence
of the mists and myths of ether -
the heart's eye
pierced by the laser of amber truth

emerging atlantis, watery
each cosmic thread split from the white
into the multitudinous spectrals
of blood and soul

i - induced
by the ineffable -
ancient hands and sighs
of love's persistent mid-wife

alive again

58. the unpardonable sin

Strewn along the
pathway of her soul -
anemones and orchids
fugues and counterpoints

Tune to the
fragrance - Tune!

Taste the A!
With your bow –
Do it – look up and smile
Dazzle them with a perfumed fugue…
A delectable pizzicato…
Remember who you are!

She looks up
bewildered

And walks
into the bog

Sinking -
mute, deaf, blind -
the chosen abandonment
of silence
and malady

gift executed

Wednesday, February 11, 2009

59. Silk Road: A New Call

we sat across from each other, familiar from a lifetime or
more of bathing in light, and I had only one
cancer business item for the agenda. We
dispensed with it
quickly. I was shocked, absolutely
shocked that he had thought I was angry at him a couple
of months ago.
and he said it was okay for me to be angry at
him even when he has cancer.
"no, I mean anytime–anytime–I've never
been angry with you." and he wondered, "irritated?
… like when I dropped the rock on your foot?"
"not even then–no–but perhaps irritated a few, very
few times."

and then we got on to why we were there, he with
his pasta and I with
my omelette.
poetry. boundary-dropping. light
filled.

and we talked as we haven't since BC
Before Cancer… perhaps as
we never have. and that's
going some.

we re-formed our writing group—"let's do
what we started the last summer, BC." and we talked
about our recent poems, about old writings, about
writings that need to be submitted, about
writings that need to be written, about
red wheel barrows against the white
snow and
cabbages and kings. we agreed that poetry is
writing's light and the
soul's fuel, a gateway at the end of a
lightpath.

and there we were, two
hours later
souls nourished, relationship nurtured and a deep
understanding of the
shadow
that hovers over
our lives, his life—
but the rest of us see it and join him to the best
of our ability. And I felt
his singular journey.
in mine. you are not allowed
to go until I've gone… that's the way I planned it. you were
planned—
planned—
planned. i keep this in my head, of
course. he needs to know and bear
none
of my singular journey.

and we talked music—
which goes without saying—nuanced triplets, the
stuff that comes from the spheres, the language of
light. our minds leaping
back and
forth
across the boundaries of time. our minds so
always able to go so far beyond time. did we play a little too
much with those
boundaries, i wonder? i would never
have led you in that direction if I'd known this
direction
was ahead. in spite of the joys and
illuminations you've given
me, i'd have bowed out if someone had only told me how
much, how long, how
dangerously you'd suffer.

and then, as we're finishing, because time calls us
back, i squint just a little to look at
my son Aslan, and i
see. it's a
soul-seeing. i must
grapple with it.
our relationship has morphed. i'm called to move into a new
role on his silk road.
Mohini calls in a new way.

it has something to do with not being
mother and son, with being
equals somehow, as though everything
is stripped away except the souls. there's oneness and
separateness
within the pure and dazzling light of
oneness. and I know, deeply perceive—I have to do
whatever i have to
do with absolutely no
agenda. i have to drop whatever
agenda I have
left.
he needs an agenda-less
companion.

i will still bow to time.

for the time
being. it will be only
a passing
glance from
now
on. in the six degrees of
light. and the multiple
dimensions.

60. chaconnes

are they memories...
or auguries?
these sensations that seep in from my shoulder
where they rest... or tap... and carry on while
I write while they take over first of all
my neck on the right and then fill that ear
so landing in that mystical musical poetical part
of my brain will open...
the chaconne of all chaconnes plays
iTunes myTunes yourTunes
GodTunes
until that odd quiet
section chaconne-particle comes and I feel
the master creating that slumbering scale that
as it builds and wakens takes
me away

Away in the power of the hands at one with
piano I
understand –
I am swept away
where time is nothing no
thing.

these fleeting moments
are not memories nor auguries but
capsules living between here and there
there and here—
and I am nothing more nor less than blessed
connected by music and of course the chaconne of all chaconnes –
the chaconne where listener, artist, guests are wordless.
I realize the
exact spot in my brain where
affinity dwells...
music consumes
the tangible, as it is and
always shall be
God's greatest gift

a brilliant red cardinal alights
on the scarlet maple, whistles and
competes with the forcefulness
of the finale
I see that it is in fact a beginning.

61. suppose

Suppose for a brief moment -
Suppose...
it were true
that two people share the same soul
if they love

Have I then crowded, shoved -
Stifled your soul?

Held my hand
over your soul's mouth...
spoken for it...
breathed for it...
yearned for it.

But I was
    lonely
    desirous
wanting more from outside.

And I found it inside
where, after the long and brooding struggle, I came home to rest
within the ample breast of silence
and the waiting lap of beyond.

I could ask one more time
    if you would come -
O taste and see...
i could ask one more time...

or not -
having so many times
and in so many ways
and in so many places
visited
    the answer.

62. winter sun

slicing through time,
precision-lasering, ener-
vating the dull, the dismal,
banishing them briefly and
slapping awake the faces of botany and human-
ity, until we sense the
coursing of blood through our veins, we notice
you, at last,
in the red surges *of* our surroundings
we feel it, this
happiness, this
joy in our re-birthing, re-bonding
with you,
the winter sun,
slicing through
time, on the wings of reds and yellows
and greens, the flushes of
awakening

63. fugue

i am your son and your
horizon—im
mutable, in
scrutable, un
finished
eternally contra
puntal, hidden in his
Great Fugue
for
ever resur
recting a
renaissance

VIII. to each, home

64. how am i to explain the rainforest?

the reality of and reason for the personal Apolalypse: for Theodora, Henry, Ben and Claudia

I am in a lush, humid rainforest—
everything is wholly
safe. a green honeycreeper calls and six scarlet macaws
laugh. I see flashes of ruby feathers in the light flickering
through the leaves. and they're
gone, their laughter lingering just over the deep, deep blue
Amazon.

The air is dense, warmly magnetic…
crackly.

There is no time.

I slip down to the river's edge, toes in the now turquoise water,
heels slipping forward in the mucky
sand. Am I the gently undulating river? I dive and swim
back to stand at the edge. I cannot afford to be
killed. Piranhas and anacondas swim
past. I am not
afraid.

I am swimmer – alone, calm, at one with everything I can see, hear, feel.

There is no time.

Predators gone, I have a sense. It comes from the Amazon. It calls silently. It's all inside my brain. I lean into the river, my face, eyes open, looking into blue blur, dead dross. Tangled, I swing my arms until I feel deepdown sleek fur. I am to do this. With astounding force, I lift out paws, patterns, tail, ears, teeth – a hefty, handsome animal, parts assembled. I hold it
lovingly. Paws around my neck, it looks up at me in powerful affinity.

Piazzolla plays a quiet
tango.

There is no time.

We continue our embrace in the purest love. Kinship. Silvery hide. Large
lavender spots. Incredible sleekness. Safe paws larger than
my hands. Head and height, slightly more than mine. Supernatural beauty. We lie down together, heads touching as we look at the steady clouds.

And the lion shall lie down with the lamb. 'Who are you?' I ask. 'We Aslans
are,' he says. 'We Aslans are
everywhere, to be discovered where the landscape meets the
sky. And where the water meets the
exact horizon.'

There is no time.

I awake from my dream-travel. I am
alone, knowing. 'My Ocelot," I cry.
'Tell me how to find you! And you
must teach me, teach me... how am I to
explain,
how am I to explain?' The Amazon has
disappeared. I cry. How am I to explain to the
younger ones that

All is safe. all is not as it
appears. All is Now and Now is
One. And fear and time are
illusions.

There is no time.

A roar parts the sky and disappears into the
streets and alleys of my
city. He is always
here – by my fireplace, in my
bookcase, in the
streets and lakes and parks, with
meadowlarks and sharks. I have an
explanation to formulate and
deliver before I
go.

There is no time!

65. at one

an other-son-of-woman, staring at death, said to me
I am at one with the holy spirit and I am
content.
and I knew he was at peace and I saw that
peace is the state of being at
one

at-one-ment, content-ment
not alone but
all one

and we talk and chatter about peace and how to achieve it and
how it should be
world peace, oh yes, world peace we say
and never see it, nor truly conceive it.

peace, being known as a river, is
only and always one-directional, moving in its one
direction from one to
all
and from community to
the world
it cannot flow otherly, it flows
motherly, increasing exponentially
exceptionally—
available, unintrusive, continually
emptying itself

peace, being a spiritual condition, passes
all understanding, all formulas, all
packaging, bartering, enforcement...
offered generously to the soul and never to
the ego

for peace is not achieved, nor is it
given out...

Peace is succumbed to.

and so peace is fleeting, a glimpseform in
this life, a
promise, a beckoning, a remembrance of
home

it comes fully and finally and utterly
at death

it is, this song we hear in life-fragments, the door
of home whispering so
softly, lovingly... welcome
welcome home to ever
lasting peace.

This book is dedicated to the two people who have been my poetry companions for what seems like forever. Poems are like shipwrecks or coral reefs. The lover, wanting to find treasures, retrieve and unravel, must dive deep, with an oxygen supply. This is what my two dear friends and I do. It's a rare thing. I dedicate this book to these two soulfriends, Evelyn Dunsmore and my son, on the other side of time, Glenn Peirson.

are you there?

are you there?
do you hear me knock at your door?
do you see me glance, then ignore?
are you there?

I walk often by your window, whether
on foot or in thought, and you turn, looking
through the juniper and maple reflections on the
glass, blue and green, white puffy clouds, and on the
sill the pretty quaint bouquet – i know the shop. i fear
you can't see through the reflections – i live in
the world of time.

you stop singing and turn from the piano, we
are blind to each other in this long
separation and yet...
yet you turn to sing again, the song we loved before
grief stole my voice... the song of Ely and Queen's Hall
on this plane. "Who calls there so like a stranger?" you
sing in the tenor i've known for bottomless
eons. And then you sing, "Go
from my window,
go."

And i
go, as i know i must, for there are edges
that cannot be traversed...
even by song.

are you there?
i turn around.

*~~ and there are times then Tennyson drops in to quote a stanza
from "Maud (Part II)" to remind us:*

A shadow flits before me,
Not thou, but like to thee:
Ah Christ, that it were possible
For one short hour to see
The souls we loved, that they might tell us
What and where they be.

Dear reader,

We hope you enjoyed reading *Orchids & Neurons*. Please take a moment to leave a review, even if it's a short one. Your opinion is important to us.

Discover more books by Ellyn Peirson at
https://www.nextchapter.pub/authors/ellyn-peirson

Want to know when one of our books is free or discounted? Join the newsletter at http://eepurl.com/bqqB3H

Best regards,
Ellyn Peirson and the Next Chapter Team

Orchids & Neurons
ISBN: 978-4-86751-271-5

Published by
Next Chapter
1-60-20 Minami-Otsuka
170-0005 Toshima-Ku, Tokyo
+818035793528
21th July 2021